SUN

Francis Spencer

A Crabtree Seedlings Book

Table of Contents

The Star in Our Solar System......4
Sun Stats and Facts......10
Heat and Light for Life......16
Glossary......23
Index......23

The Star in Our Solar System

Scientists believe our **universe** has billions of solar systems. A solar system is made up of a star and all the objects that **orbit** around it.

A star is a ball of burning gases.

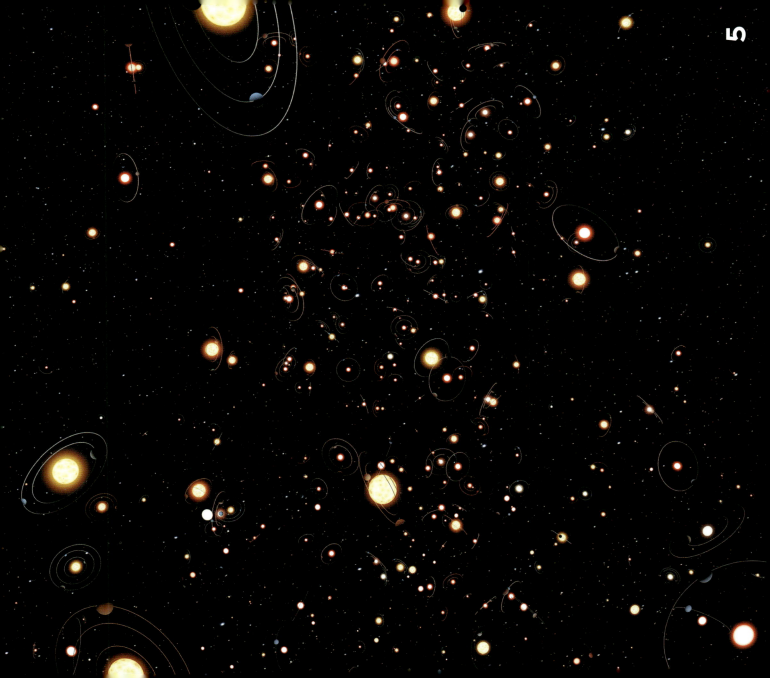

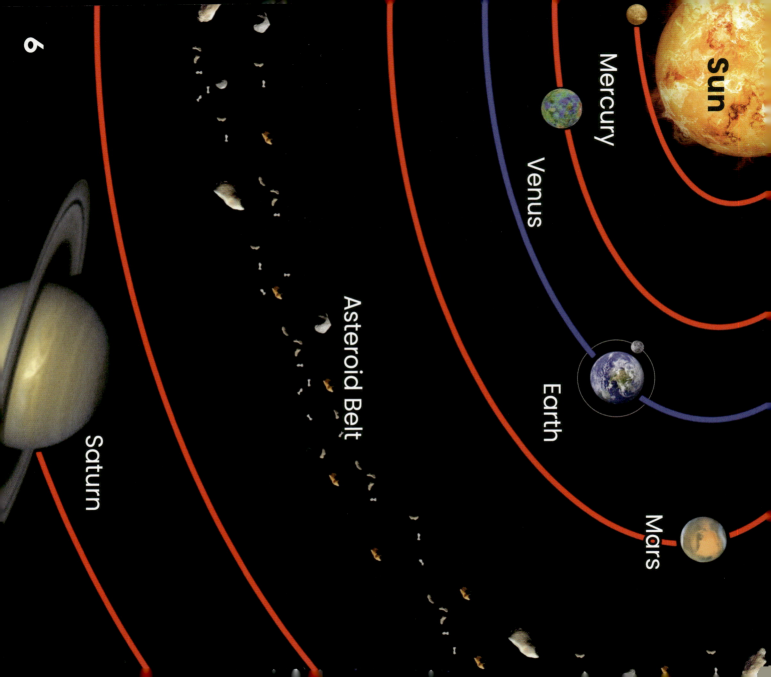

In our solar system, eight planets orbit a star we call the Sun.

The Sun's **gravity** holds all of these planets in their orbit. Other space objects, such as asteroids, also orbit the Sun.

Earth is the third planet from the Sun in our solar system.

Uranus

Jupiter

Neptune

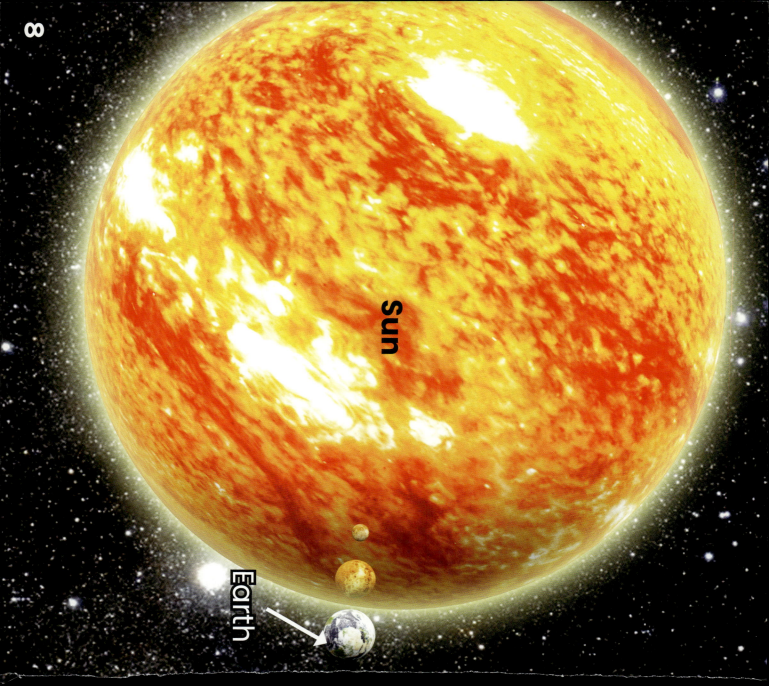

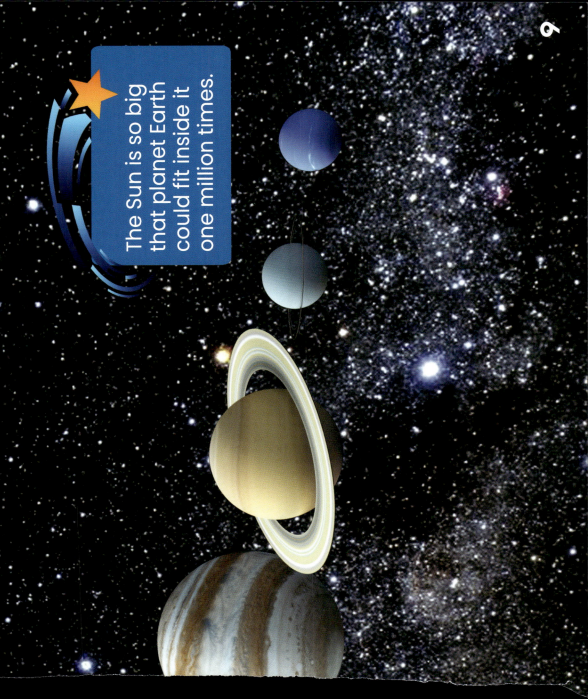

The Sun's gravity is so strong because of its massive size and weight.

The Sun is so big that planet Earth could fit inside it one million times.

Sun Stats and Facts

The Sun is made up of burning gases.

The temperature on the surface of the Sun is about 10,000° Fahrenheit (5,538° Celsius).

The Sun's **atmosphere** is called the corona. The temperature of the corona can get as high as 3.5 million degrees Fahrenheit (1.9 million degrees Celsius).

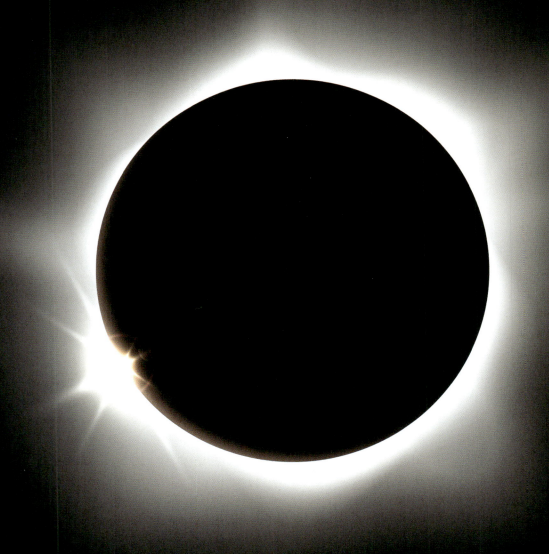

The corona can only be seen during a total solar eclipse.

The Sun's gases are always moving. **Solar** flares explode as hot streams of burning gas.

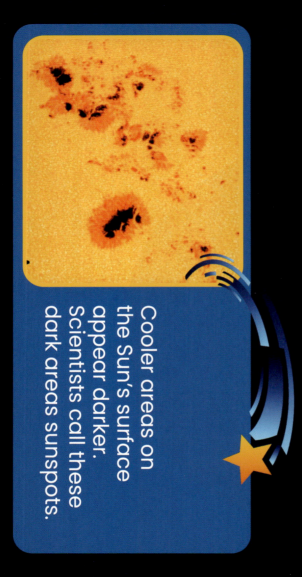

Cooler areas on the Sun's surface appear darker. Scientists call these dark areas sunspots.

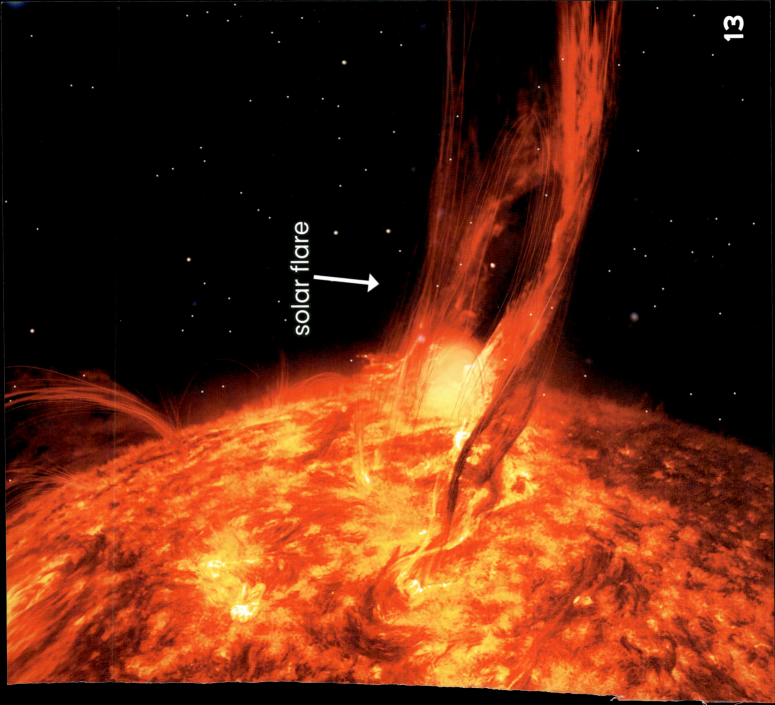

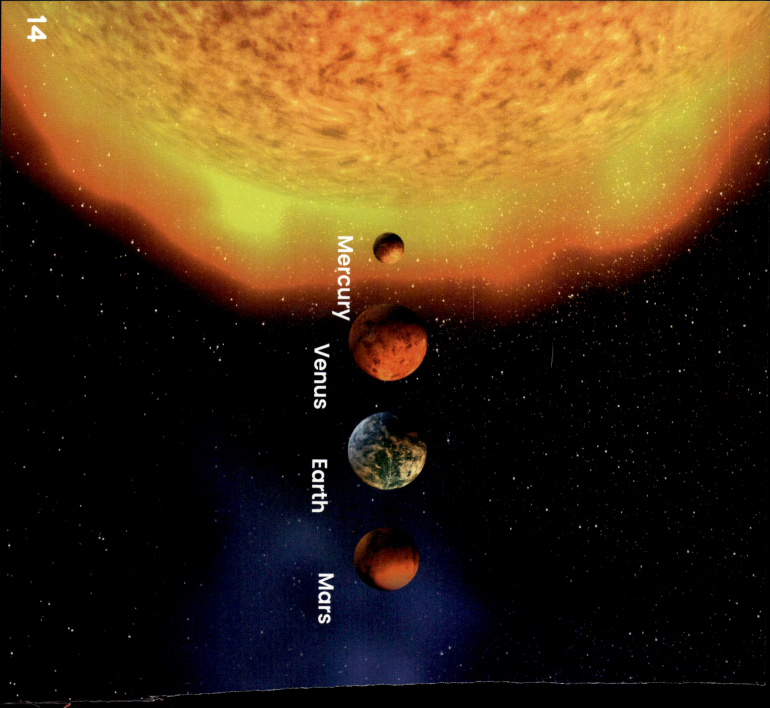

The Sun is 93 million miles (150 million kilometers) away from Earth. Light from the Sun takes about eight minutes to reach Earth.

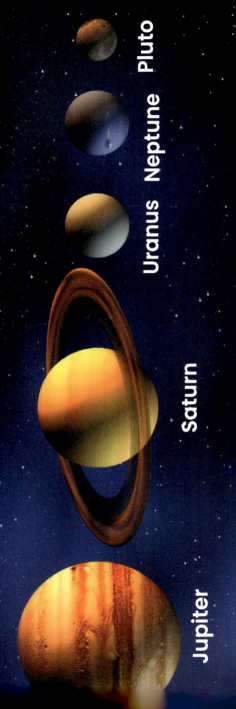

Jupiter
Saturn
Uranus
Neptune
Pluto

It takes about 5.3 hours for the Sun's light to reach the dwarf planet Pluto.

Heat and Light for Life

Life on Earth depends on the Sun's heat, light, and **energy**.

Green Zone

Earth

Earth is the perfect distance from the Sun. It is positioned in a green zone. This keeps Earth the right temperature for us to live.

Without sunlight, plants could not grow. People and animals would starve.

Lucky for us, Earth has liquid water. This is also needed for life.

Plants need energy from the Sun to make their food. People and animals need energy from plants and other animals.

We can use sunlight to make solar energy. Solar energy is **renewable**.

Solar collectors use energy from sunlight to heat air or water inside houses.

The Sun is about four and a half billion years old. Scientists believe it has enough energy to exist for another five billion years.

Glossary

atmosphere (AT-muhss-fihr): Outermost layer of gases.

energy (EN-ur-jee): The ability to do work.

gravity (GRAV-uh-tee): The force that holds the planets in our solar system in their orbit.

orbit (OR-bit): To travel in an invisible path around a larger object, such as a planet or star.

renewable (ri-NOO-uh-buhl): From a source that can never be used up.

solar (SOH-lur): To do with the Sun.

universe (YOO-nuh-vurss): Everything that exists in space, including Earth.

Index

corona 10, 11
Earth 6–9, 14–18
energy 16, 19, 20, 22
gases 4, 10, 12
gravity 7, 9
orbit 4, 7
planets 7
solar 4, 7, 11, 12, 13, 20, 21
star 4, 7
universe 4

School-to-Home Support for Caregivers and Teachers

This book helps children grow by letting them practice reading. Here are a few guiding questions to help the reader build his or her comprehension skills. Possible answers appear here in red.

Before Reading

- **What do I think this book is about?** I think this book is about our Sun. I think this book is about why the Sun is important.
- **What do I want to learn about this topic?** I want to learn how hot the Sun gets. I want to learn more about the relationship between Earth and the Sun.

During Reading

- **I wonder why...** I wonder why there are sunspots on the Sun's surface. I wonder why light from the Sun takes about eight minutes to reach Earth.

After Reading

- **What details did I learn about this topic?** I have learned that the Sun is about four and a half billion years old. I have learned that the Sun is made up of burning gases.
- **Read the book again and look for the glossary words.** I see the word *atmosphere* on page 10, and the word *energy* on page 16. The other glossary words are found on page 23.
- **What have I learned so far?** I have learned that Earth is the perfect distance from the Sun, making Earth the right temperature to support life. I have learned that energy from the Sun is called renewable because it can never be used up.

Library and Archives Canada Cataloguing in Publication

CIP available at Library and Archives Canada

Library of Congress Cataloging-in-Publication Data

CIP available at Library of Congress

Crabtree Publishing Company
www.crabtreebooks.com 1-800-387-7650

Written by: Francis Spencer
Production coordinator and Prepress technician: Tammy McGarr
Print coordinator: Katherine Berti

Printed in the U.S.A./CG20210915/01202

Published in the United States
Crabtree Publishing
347 Fifth Ave.
Suite 1402-145
New York, NY 10016

Published in Canada
Crabtree Publishing
616 Welland Ave.
St. Catharines, Ontario
L2M 5V6

Print book version produced jointly with Blue Door Education in 2022

Content produced and published by Blue Door Education, Melbourne Beach FL USA. This title Copyright Blue Door Education. All rights reserved. No part of this book may be reproduced or utilized in any form or by any means, electronic or mechanical including photocopying, recording, or by any information storage and retrieval system without permission in writing from the publisher.

PHOTO CREDITS:
Cover ©solarseven, star graphic header ©Gleb Guralnyk, pages 2-3 © Dr. Thomas Spaeter /Shutterstock.com, page 5 ©ESO/M. Kornmesser, http://www.eso.org/public/images/eso1204a/; page 6 ©ktynzq /Shutterstock.com; pages 8, 9 © Bobboz /Shutterstock.com; page 11 © Lonely /Shutterstock.com; page 12 courtesy of NASA, SDO, page 13 shutterstock.com; page 14-15 ©Orla /Shutterstock.com; page 16-17 ©Hannu Viitanen i Dreamstime.com. Page 18 ©Filip Fuxa /Shutterstock.com; page 19 ©LSkywalker /Shutterstock.com; page 21 ©manfredxy /Shutterstock.com; page 22 ©Triff /Shutterstock.com.

24